From Alig to Half Parisian

OrangeBooks Publication

1st Floor, Rajhans Arcade, Mall Road, Kohka, Bhilai, Chhattisgarh 490020

Website: **www.orangebooks.in**

© Copyright, 2025, Author

All rights reserved. No part of this book may be reproduced, stored in a retrieval system, or transmitted, in any form by any means, electronic, mechanical, magnetic, optical, chemical, manual, photocopying, recording or otherwise, without the prior written consent of its writer.

First Edition, 2025

ISBN: 978-93-6554-129-8

FROM ALIG
—— TO ——
HALF PARISIAN

HAZIQ NASEER KHAN

OrangeBooks Publication
www.orangebooks.in

Preface

Life is based on experience; the more you have, the better. Sometimes, different experiences can untie many knots in your life, releasing your hidden potential. Travelling can be very instrumental in this process. Unfortunately, people often misunderstand its core value these days. Simply taking pictures and staying in luxury hotels does no good. However, observing the systems of more progressive societies and drawing inspiration from admirable individuals can elevate your maturity and deepen your understanding.

"From Alig to Half Parisian" tells the story of personal growth, that begins in the historic halls of Aligarh Muslim University (AMU) and unfolds across continents, bridging two distinct cultures. It is not only a narrative of academic pursuits or traveling to new places. It's about discovering how both learning and life experiences can reveal hidden strengths and teach valuable lessons. This book invites you to reflect on how stepping beyond familiar boundaries can reshape ambitions and bring deeper meaning to journey, turning an ordinary path into an extraordinary voyage.

"Life is a journey from point a to point b, some people make stories between these two points while others read them."

The Author

To my family, especially my parents
(Abu ji & Didilalo), for their guidance, love and support.

Acknowledgement

I would like to acknowledge and thank my brother, Basiq Naseer Khan, for his guidance and support in reviewing.

I would also like to thank Asif Raza for his suggestions during the review process.

Chapter - 1

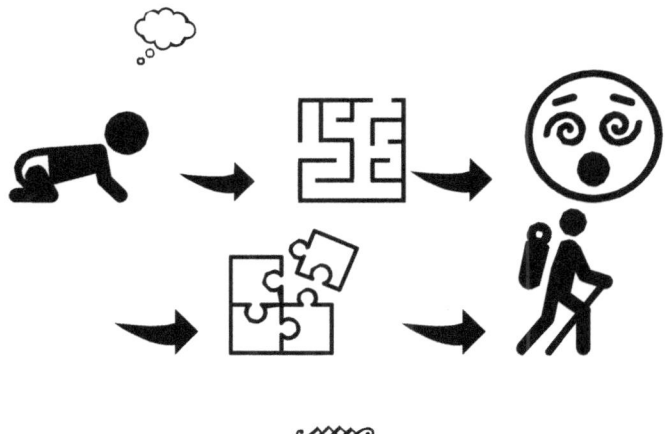

It was the mid of summer, marking the start of our second year of college. Students were returning from their vacations, filling the corridors and lawns with energy and excitement, the air buzzing with conversations and laughter. As I walked past room 303 on the third floor of Habib Hall, Mujtaba called out to me as he was longing to show me something on his smartphone. Displayed on the screen was a photograph of four students from our alma mater, Aligarh Muslim University (AMU), proudly celebrating their achievement of securing scholarships to study in Hungary. Considering the vast student body of AMU, which enrolls around 30,000 students, recognizing anyone was a challenge. However, I immediately noticed Amir in one corner of the picture. He was tall and skinny with a dark brown skin tone, one year senior to us, and lived in the same residence hall. I had seen him not long ago, performing the AMU Tarana (anthem) at the annual hall event. His impression was that of an average student who was too active in student politics and conspicuously present at every *chai tapri* (tea stall), from Chungi Point to the streets of Jamalpur. Both Mujtaba and I were taken aback that someone whom we had underestimated could achieve such a distinction. His achievements, on the other hand, also kindled hope within us, the possibility that we too could emulate his success and secure an opportunity to study abroad. Lost in thought, we found ourselves drifting in a daydream, much like "Sheikh Chilli". I was imagining the lush green parks surrounded by medieval European architecture, with a cold breeze gently waving on our faces.

So far, we had attended a few conferences and seminars held at Kennedy Hall to lure students to study abroad, but the success of Amir had a major hit on our minds. Inspired by his success, Mujtaba and I ventured on a new journey, driven by our ambition to pursue international academic opportunities. Our previous year's goal of passing the National Medical Entrance Exam, aka NEET, had changed. Realizing the high failure rate among candidates, we decided to align with the majority and set our sight on a different path. With our new goal set, we were clueless about how to proceed. So, we dived into researching the application requirements, and the first thing we encountered was the term "CV," a term neither we nor our ancestors were familiar with. This acronym, short for "Curriculum Vitae," was initially puzzling, but further investigation revealed it to be a document detailing a person's education, skills, and achievements. In short, it was what people typically seek in matchmaking, but in this case, it was intended to be presented in a highly technical format.

As second-year bachelor's students with seemingly fewer scientific skills than science enthusiasts of the 18th century, we were stumped about what to include. Turning to Google for enlightenment, we decided to build our skills or, at the very least, get an official recognition for the purpose of studying abroad. We began with the simpler task of engaging in co-curricular activities, though this section of the CV was as confusing as a modern multi-sectioned trash bin, leaving many uncertainties about what and where to list items.

In our pursuit of securing an internship to strengthen our CV, we faced repeated rejections and excuses from the heads of the chemistry department. Not deterred and not seeing any option left, I took matters into my own hands. I convinced my friend and classmate Asim, who was initially disinterested in studying abroad, to collaborate on a research article. He had some experience in publishing, so it seemed a promising start. The question of what to write in the article was answered during our 5th semester's lab session when we conducted our experiment using a UV-visible spectrophotometer. The idea struck in my mind, to write about this experiment and aim for publication in an obscure national journal. I began drafting the text, while Asim worked on the graphs and data analysis. When we finished drafting the article, it was time to cover the publication cost and that hit us so hard that we had to approach Mujtaba and another friend for financial contributions, offering to include their names in the article as co - authors.

In the meantime, we began preparing for the TOEFL exam, an English proficiency test. During the summer, the AMU alumni association funds a program called Sir Syed Global Scholar Award (SSGA), which sponsors English proficiency tests and also offers guidance for students in their foreign applications. Mujtaba and I, as enthusiastic as we were, submitted our applications early. Meanwhile, another classmate, Wajid, also became interested and joined the queue of foreign applicants. On the last day to apply for SSGA, we urged him to apply urgently. He and Mujtaba tackled the application right off the bat and submitted it just fifteen minutes before the deadline. We then awaited the results, hopeful for ourselves, and admiring Wajid's last-minute effort. Surprisingly, he was the only one among us who received the call for the interview, which he qualified for and was later declared as the selected candidate, exemplifying the notion of providence, what Allah has decreed for you will come to pass.

Months later, Mujtaba and I paid out of pocket to book the TOEFL examination slot in Delhi. Wajid, having taken the test a week earlier than us, was content with his performance. Our exam was scheduled for Sunday morning, so we had to leave for Delhi the day before. We stayed with Mujtaba's friends in Old Delhi, and while they were inquiring about the exam, we felt a bit hesitant to tell them. It felt very naive and shy to talk about going abroad, as it was not a very common thing to do at that time. We were also preoccupied with another concern since our physical chemistry exam was scheduled for the following day. We reached the TOEFL exam center early in the morning and outside the center, there were numerous students, some with their parents, some already elated as though they were already swaying in the Alps of Switzerland, and others, like us, preoccupied with the thought of potentially losing 13,000 rupees if the exam turned out poorly.

The entrance to the exam hall resembled the lobby of a cozy boutique hotel, complete with comfortable couches and a mesmerizing fish tank.

We were taken to different rooms individually to take an oath of confidentiality, with an audio recording, not to disclose the exam paper. It was like giving testimony before a judge in a courtroom. Next, some young staff members escorted us to the exam hall very kindly. The atmosphere there felt slightly chaotic and crowded, much like a bustling call center. We were then assigned seats equipped with a computer, headset with a microphone, several multicolored A4-sized sheets of paper and a pencil. The TOEFL English proficiency test consisted of four sections: reading, listening, speaking, and writing. As I began the exam with the reading section, I misjudged the time allotted for each question, thinking I had 5 minutes per question instead of the actual 1 or 2 minutes. I worked through the questions comfortably until, at question sixteen, I glanced at the clock and felt a wave of panic, only 2 or 3 minutes remained to tackle fourteen more questions in the first section. In a frantic rush, I skimmed through the paragraphs at lightning speed, finishing a mere few seconds before the time for that section ran out. Disappointment washed over me as I was unsure of my answers, I stood up from my chair, ready to leave and regretting my mistake and decision. In that moment of reflection, I thought to myself, this is the decree of Allah. With a deep breath, I sat down to face the remaining three sections, curious to see what fate had in store.

Stepping out of the exam center, I confided in Mujtaba about running out of time, fearing I wouldn't even score sixty. There was not enough time to regret it as we had to leave for Aligarh the same day in the evening and prepare for the physical chemistry exam the next day. Two weeks later, the email with my results popped up on my laptop screen. I was scared to death. As I hesitantly opened the email, to my astonishment, the results showed I had scored 93, so far, the highest in our group. Overwhelmed with gratitude, I thanked Allah for this unexpected blessing that served as a boon to my candidacy. Once again, destiny had defied logic.

During this period of preparations, representatives from various Finnish universities accompanied by some financial advisors visited Aligarh Muslim University (AMU). They arrived with posters and pamphlets, promoting the opportunity to study the different English-speaking courses in their country. I collected many pamphlets and adorned the walls of my room at Habib Hall with clippings from these papers. Whenever someone visited my room, their first glance was drawn to the three posters, that I had arranged in descending order, beginning with 'Study in Canada' and finishing with 'Study in Switzerland'. At that time, the idea of studying abroad was like a beautiful dream, an enchanting vision as the cold breeze of the Swiss Alps, but the reality was as daunting as enduring the dining meals in the residence halls. Yet, we persevered our enthusiasm, for there was no greater motivation for us than the prospect of studying and experiencing life at a European university. Finally, with a lot of effort and muddling through, we managed to get an article published, completed some online courses, engaged in co-curricular activities, and compiled a mediocre -looking CV, but it was a CV nonetheless.

Our next goal was to write a motivation letter, or what we referred to as a Statement of Purpose (S.O.P). It took me more than a month to compose my own S.O.P. and tailor it for each master's program. Since no previous templates were available and AI's like ChatGPT were still in their embryonic stage at that time, we had no choice but to start from scratch.

After all the other documentation, it was time to obtain the all-important letters of recommendation. Seeking to make a strong impression, we first approached our senior professors, but they hardly recognized us and promptly declined. Feeling disheartened, we sought guidance from the assistant and associate professors, and to our relief and delight, they proved to be far more approachable and supportive. When I asked for the recommendation, one of the assistant professors simply said, "You draft it, I'll review and sign it." Hearing this, I couldn't help but smile to myself, it was finally time to write some positive things about ourselves.

Despite receiving positive responses from most of our faculty members, some professors were reluctant and even discouraged knowing about our plans to study abroad. They favored pursuing national-level exams like JRF/NET as better and more intellectual options instead. Qualifying for these exams will only help us secure admission to a Ph.D. program at local universities, potentially with a scholarship for a limited duration. But when asked about placement opportunities in India, their sole recommendation was employment at private universities. However, these positions often come with minimal salaries, heavy workloads, and temporary job contracts, making them less appealing.

The likelihood of PhD students in India securing assistant professor positions is as uncommon as spotting solid yellow beans in a dining hall's dal curry. They perceived studying abroad as merely an escape from real hard work, a perception that seems deeply rooted in naivete rather than verity.

With the beginning of the final year of our bachelor's degree, the anticipation for postgraduate opportunities grew. The University of Eastern Finland was our top choice, given that students from our Chemistry and Physics departments had previously secured scholarships for their master's programs. Another option was the "Stipendium Hungaricum" scholarship for studying in Hungary, which had been previously obtained by Amir, the same guy whose selection bolstered us to follow the same dream.

This phase of sending applications abroad faced a setback when our university came under attack by the infringing elements of society, which led to violent confrontations between students and police. The law enforcement, falling short in their duties, worsened the situation by using force against the protesting students on campus. Many were injured and arrested, with some suffering severe injuries to the extent of amputation. The administration, particularly the Vice-Chancellor (VC) of that time, Tanveer Maqsood, showed a distressing lack of support and empathy towards students, fueling further protests and leading to the university's temporary shutdown. The day before the closure, students started protesting all night outside the VC's lodge. Some students were chasing the car of the VC, demanding accountability for his lack of management and consideration.

The closure coincided with an internet shutdown in Kashmir, which severely hindered our application process which was set to begin in late December. Despite the uncertainty, we resolved to return to the university in January. We managed to book air tickets but faced the dilemma of finding accommodation since all the hostels were closed indefinitely. Upon arrival, we found the hostel doors sealed. Being an "Alig" means being resourceful and finding creative solutions, colloquially termed as "Jugaad." We carefully peeled off the seal from the lock to gain entry. Whenever we left, we would reapply the bandage over the lock to maintain appearances, making it appear unruffled and keeping us above suspicion.

The once bustling hostel was looking like a haunted building with the souls of students roaming around. Over 400 rooms stood vacant, their emptiness exuding an eerie desolation. The only exception was a student from Azamgarh, who had stayed behind throughout the closure. His stay and survival during this period were no less than a miracle due to his weak physical stature. In this atmosphere of solitude, our primary concern shifted back to the scholarship applications. Our naivety and skepticism led us to meticulously scrutinize every detail, fearing even the slightest error which consequently led to more work as we were sleeping late through the night to complete the applications. Tired of committing repeated mistakes, the feeling of quitting was also very obvious.

Eventually, the university resumed to normal, and the competition for European scholarships intensified. Students from various departments, including Botany and

Zoology, began applying for master's programs in Chemistry, which seemed an unlikely transition. As we proceeded with various applications, the "Hungarian" one proved to be far from straightforward, requiring extensive documentation and time. After submitting our applications with all the required documents to the embassy, we awaited the results which were due in March. In our quest for educational advancement, we cast a wide net, applying for scholarships worldwide. Applications for countries like Thailand and China necessitated thorough medical testing, requiring us to undergo medical X-ray scans, which were perceived to be less unusual than HIV tests. We had to explain to the employee at JNMC Hospital in an extremely awkward and embarrassing manner as to why we needed such a test.

As the responses to our applications began coming in, the start was somewhat smooth since we were selected by some English universities for self-funded positions with tuition fees amounting to £25,000 per year. This financial shock was followed by another harsh blow, leading to extreme disappointment after being rejected by an institute in Thailand. The country, primarily known for its tourism, apparently did not find our application compelling enough to grant us admission. This left us feeling dejected, questioning the value of our profiles in the eyes of European universities.

March had arrived, and with it grew our anticipation for the results of the scholarships, especially the Hungarian one. The announcement's exact date was in the air but anticipated at any time. During the same month, a conference was held in the Department of Chemistry right after lunch. While we were listening, or at least pretending to be attentive to the talks being delivered, a message flashed in our chemistry WhatsApp group. Someone had posted the list of candidates nominated for the Hungarian scholarship. My heart raced, and I felt a pound load of stress on my head, the conference room felt like an empty hall for that moment. We scrolled down the list, searching for our names. With each passing second, the inevitability of our absence from the list sank in. A collective disappointment shadowed the room, but the most disheartening news was yet to break. It was about a student named Salman from the Botany department who had astonishingly been selected for the Master's course in Chemistry at a Hungarian university. The pain of failure spread like a pandemic among the applicants and this news made it worse. I turned to Wajid, whose face was etched with profound disbelief. I offered him some words of consolation; I said to him "This is Allah's will. He does as He pleases. Perhaps Allah has something better for us. Let us maintain hope and faith that we will ultimately succeed on our path, Inshallah."

As time marched on, the likelihood of landing a scholarship seemed to fade, one rejection followed another. The arrival of each notification email felt like a mini cardiac arrest as we were petrified by the continuous rejections. Weeks passed, and the buzz about studying abroad spread throughout the student body. Curious peers approached us, eager to learn about the application process. We were always willing to assist, but upon hearing about the requirements, many would hesitantly respond, "*Mujhse nahi hoga bhai, aap pehle kar lijiye ga,*" which translates to "I can't do it, brother. You go ahead." Despite their reservations, we encouraged them to apply, but some students were taking shortcuts, making fake certificates, and lying in their CVs about their technical skills. Asim, the article guy, was one of the recruits to join the growing pool of applicants. Our application efforts intensified again, particularly for self-financed Master's courses in England. However, the overwhelming cost became a significant concern, as the budget requirement was beyond what we might have inherited from our ancestors.

It was the beginning of January 2020 and our last semester had just started; the news of pandemic was grooming around everywhere. Our professors were skeptical and unsure, if regular classes would continue as the news of another university shutdown loomed overhead. Our anxiety peaked when, just a week into the semester, the university was closed once again and students were asked to vacate from the hostels. Thankfully, by this point, we had managed to complete all A, B, and C of our application essentials.

Just in the nick of time, before the pandemic unleashed its full chaos, we had pinned our hopes on the University of Paris-Saclay and the University of Burgundy, both located in France. Those applications felt like our last ticket for studying abroad. For approximately one month after the lockdown, there was a pause as all the available university applications were closed. We were all in a dilemma about our future as we sat in our homes comfortably undergoing trouble-free online exams from our cozy beds and couches. The curfew over the country seemed like a dimming hope. Everything went into a state of dormancy; we were just waiting for the heartbreaking emails from the universities we had applied to, which started with "We regret to inform you" and ended with "We hope you will find another position." In this period of stress and losing hope, just after a few months, as I sifted through my emails, my heart skipped a beat. I received a message from the University of Burgundy confirming my admission to two of their master's courses with a scholarship. I read the email over and over to make sure it wasn't a mirage, ensuring I wasn't being delusional. After being content it was real, I called up my friends to share the news.

While I was cherishing the joy, Mujtaba didn't receive a response, which we sadly interpreted as a silent refusal. Mujtaba was engulfed by stress, while my other peers, Wajid and Asim, were selected. It was a bittersweet moment for us, as one of our friends didn't get selected. We also forecasted that it would be yet another marathon to run, fulfilling all the requirements during the worst period of the pandemic looming above us. Mujtaba and I were also selected for the master's course in chemistry at the University of Paris-Saclay, but there was no scholarship available to cover our living expenses. The self-finance option, despite the tuition fee waiver and the university's good reputation and ranking, was not enough for us to take a loan from the bank.

With our acceptance at the University of Burgundy, we began to realize the massive amount of work required to obtain the visa, especially during the COVID-19 pandemic when curfews and quarantines were ubiquitous. Our final semester results had not been declared yet, so we could not include our degrees for the visa applications, which was a prerequisite. As COVID-19 cases were increasing in India and globally, embassies temporarily shuttered their doors in New Delhi. Confined to our homes, we feared any misfortune that might affect our visa application process. The visa process also required a Non-Objection Certificate (NOC) from different offices of "Campus France" located in various cities across India. We began applying for it, but progress stalled as we lacked the crucial document of our final academic transcript. After some days, it became very obvious to us that we were not going to seek the visa until all the documents were obtained.

In the meantime, when everybody was stuck in limbo and waiting for embassies to open, many groups on WhatsApp were formed to share information and connect with other students who were planning to study abroad. Asim, Wajid and I created our own group "France ka shishay" (pupils of France) and also joined other whatsapp groups as well. It was through these new connections that I met Hamza, another Kashmiri boy who had completed his master's in Chemistry at Jawaharlal Nehru University (JNU) in Delhi. From our first phone conversation, he struck to me as a competitive and a slightly narcissistic kind of person, always keen to boast about his achievements. He had secured admission in M2 master's course in Chemistry at University of Paris Saclay, supported by a scholarship worth of 10,000 euros per annum.

{Unlike India, the French master's programme is divided into two parts: M1 and M2. Each part leads to a separate diploma, and together, they constitute a complete master's degree. Indian students with a master's degree can directly enroll in the M2 course, as they already fulfill the minimum European Credit Transfer System (ECTS) required by the course.}

I had been selected for the M1 program at the same university in the same course. This master's course offered at the University of Paris- Saclay was funded by the European Union education program also known as Erasmus Mundus. It featured the opportunity to study in different European countries each semester. However, since I was accepted on a self-finance basis and without the mobility option, my chances of attending were very slim. I had applied for another Campus France scholarship to finance myself for this program, but my expectations were low as it was very rare to receive that grant. In the meantime, we started our process of completing the application on the online portal of Campus France for obtaining the NOC certificate, which we needed for the Visa application later.

It was my usual evening, and I was scrolling through my mailbox when a notification popped up. It was an email from the head office of Campus France in Paris about a scholarship opportunity. It felt like a stroke of luck, a rare chance that comes once in a blue moon. The email indicated that I was on the scholarship waiting list from Campus France, with the possibility of being awarded. This scholarship was for my M1 Master's program at the University of Paris-Saclay. Merely weeks later, I received an affirmative response, confirming my selection for the scholarship.

The scholarship was no less than hitting a jackpot, offering me 1,190 euros (more than 1 lakh INR) monthly for a 24-month period, including round-trip flight tickets, visa fees, and health insurance. Recalling that the first cohort of recipients in 2018 had the opportunity to meet and dine with the French President, Emmanuel Macron. I realized the prestige of this award; it was akin to France's version of the Rhodes Scholarship. Overwhelmed with gratitude, I performed "sajda-e- shukr" (Prostration) upon receiving the news. However, despite all these perks from the grant, my family's reaction was mixed, as I had already anticipated. My mother was hesitant about the idea of her son moving abroad, while my brother and my sister, having a gloomy outlook towards studying abroad, sided with her out of deep affection and concern for my well-being abroad. Despite their objections, I tried to persuade them with the financial benefits, but my mother dismissed it, saying, "May me haw rupye keh" (Don't show me the money). My father, however, supported my decision and was willing to cover my tuition fees, which were 3,600 euros annually.

Eventually, I convinced my family, though we kept the news a secret from other relatives until my departure was certain, given the pandemic's pervasive uncertainty. I still had several documents to finalize like my final transcript and the accommodation certificate was also not ready yet. On the other hand, the French embassy remained closed until the news broke in the last week of July that the embassies were reopening.

In this period, I was in contact with my coordinator at the University of Paris-Saclay, informing them about the scholarship that I had been awarded. They surprised me with the reply that I had been exempted from paying the tuition fees since my scholarship was sponsored by Campus France. This relief was like the cherry on the cake, lifting the hefty financial burden of approximately 3.5 lakh annually for tuition fees. My focus now shifted from the University of Burgundy to the University of Paris-Saclay. The application process was similar, but changing universities along with receiving a scholarship made my application easier, as I was not required to show a bank statement, unlike my peers.

When the embassy finally reopened, we headed to Delhi, where I reached out to my friends, Wajid and Asim. As Asim had a residence in Delhi, I stayed with him. During this time, we planned a trip to Aligarh to seek the intervention of a court member of the science faculty for the early release of our transcripts. We aimed to expedite the announcement of our final semester results so that we could obtain our final transcripts from the office of the AMU "controller examinations" office. However, as we were preparing to leave for Aligarh, news of the demise of Asim's grandfather in Jharkhand arrived. This event took an unexpected turn, slightly derailing our plans, but we remained resolute. We suggested that Asim accompany his mother to Jharkhand, while Wajid and I would proceed to Aligarh for the documentation process.

The next morning, we booked a cab and departed for Aligarh. Our optimism was tempered by the fact that our final results had not yet been announced, and classes in

France were starting in the next month. Upon reaching Aligarh Muslim University, we found it eerily empty due to the pandemic, with only the administrative departments operational. From the moment we arrived, I was overwhelmed with a sense of nostalgia for my Chaman (AMU). My heart ached with longing, and I often expressed this feeling to Wajid by saying that Aligarh seemed to be drawing closer to us more than ever before. The roads, buildings, trees, and our beloved chai tapri were calling to us like no other time, the emotional cry we felt was beyond words.

On the very first day, we met Khaliq Bhai, the court member from the Faculty of Science. Upon hearing our situation, he generously offered his assistance. Wajid used his motorcycle to carry me and Khaliq Bhai to the controller's office. For several days, he accompanied us to the Examination Controller's office, advocating on our behalf. The staff at the controller's office, upon learning of our admission to European universities, began to process our paperwork with personal investment, as if we were their children embarking on the journey. There was one individual, Rihan bhai, whose efforts I can never forget. He personally organized our files and documents with such care that it felt as though we had hired him specifically for this task. He was touched by our achievement, and at that time I realized the true sweetness of my alma mater. The final results were not announced yet, and the chairman himself instructed a staff member to prepare the transcript specially for us and announce the results for our chemistry batch. No matter how many cons I counted over the years, today I felt blessed to be an alumnus of this garden of knowledge, our cherished home, our Aligarh. Remarkably, we completed all our documentation in less than a week, a task nearly impossible to do at any other university in India. This is the essence of AMU, its ability to leave an indelible mark on your soul. Even if your time here is brief, its influence will stay with you for a lifetime. AMU is not just an institution, it is a bond, a family, and a legacy that will remain with you, no matter where life takes you.

We hustled to submit the documents for the visa application and completed all the paperwork. I began packing my belongings from the room no 15 of Habib Hall, books, some clothes, and many memories. Just a week later, while I was still in Aligarh, I received an envelope from the visa office. Fearing the worst due to my long beard, I braced myself for rejection. Upon opening the passport, I was thrilled to find that my student visa had been granted, and simultaneously, my flight was booked by the scholarship committee. For the first time, I felt certain that I was going to France. Meanwhile, Wajid and Asim had yet to hear from the visa office, but we were all hopeful for a positive outcome soon.

After receiving my visa confirmation, I gathered my belongings, vacated the hostel room, and bid farewell to my friends. My roommate, Imtiyaz, was at home due to the pandemic, so I inscribed a message for him on the wall: "It is not the goodbye that hurts, but the flashbacks that follow". I took some photos of my room, touched the table and chair for the last time, and noticed that the posters of my study abroad were still hanging on the wall. This was the moment I saw my dream as an Alig finally come to life. With one last glance, I bid farewell to my alma mater, carrying with me the cherished memories of a chapter now gracefully closed.

Even though my classes in France had already begun, I returned to Kashmir first to share the news and bid farewell to my relatives, neighbors, and friends. It was impossible for me to simply fly to France without any notice; otherwise, I would have had to bear the burden of my mistake, and my friends and relatives would forever consider me an infamous person.

After I shared the news of my departure with them, their reactions were a mix of joy and uncertainty. They couldn't quite grasp what I was set to achieve, as it was a degree they believed could be earned locally. Yet, they were astonished to witness the first person from our community going abroad on a full scholarship. Rumors started spreading, some thought I was going to America, others guessed Dubai, and a few speculated about a job offer. However, my close friends, aware of my destination and the scholarship amount, were pleasantly surprised. Ignoring the speculation, I continued with my preparations, which started with visiting some local clothing stores, relatives, and friends. With so little time in my hands, I began visiting each relative one by one. In Kashmiri household, it is not considered culturally appropriate to leave the host's home without eating or staying there for a night. Therefore, my aunts were leaving no chance but to feed me as if I was leaving and never coming back. My youngest aunt was very excited as I had told her several months ago about a surprise I was going to give her. Upon hearing this news, she was thrilled, and so were my cousins. During this busy schedule of mine, where I had to hop around from one relative's home to another, I went to exchange the currency since there were only a few days left until my departure. I handed over a significant amount of cash to the employee of the J&K bank, and he handed back a very thin envelope containing one 100 - euro bill along with four 50- euro bills and a receipt. I had a very spooky feeling and was also cynical and scared that I might cut or damage these super expensive paper notes.

As the clock was ticking fast for my retreat, I had begun to notice the sadness in the eyes of my mother at the thought of me being far away. She was suffering, yet she had remained silent until my departure day. On the last day, she embraced me tightly, and her crying was unlike any I had ever heard. As I was leaving, she clung to me, repeating the words "Paye chum ne kar yekh wapas," meaning "I don't know when you will come back." My emotionless face changed for a time being and I began to struggle to keep up and quickly ran into the car. My father drove me to the Srinagar airport, from where I boarded a flight to New Delhi.

I extended my stay in Delhi for a few more days to gather essential items we had identified through our itinerary and research. At that time, we were quite naive about distinguishing the truly indispensable from the utterly trivial. We reached out to our contacts and watched YouTube videos for guidance. It was surprising that a pressure cooker was highly recommended by everyone, even by people in the online videos. Our family and friends found it amusing and wondered why we couldn't just buy one in France. The idea of carrying a metal container halfway around the world seemed very bizarre to all of us. We also visited many shops in search of a lab coat and other lab accessories, as we were expecting to use them during our lab courses. We finally found a store with a few in stock, although the lab coats were as short as our T-shirts. The safety goggles were made of soft plastic with an elastic band, similar to the type used as drawstring in trousers to keep them from slipping. We also bought a pair of latex gloves, naively believing they would last us the entire year in the lab. While I was busy shopping and packing, people who had already reached France unusually began to call for bringing some stuff for themselves and at the same time discouraged me from arriving due to difficulties in studies and cultural differences. I couldn't help but wonder if their advice was genuinely well-intentioned or driven by other motives.

Finally, the day arrived for my journey from the city of monuments to the city of love. I booked an Uber and left for the airport. On the way, numerous thoughts raced through my mind, and I felt a tinge of nervousness. The weight of stress bore down on me, but my faith reassured me that Allah had the best plan for me. My Air France flight was scheduled for 11 P.M. After receiving my boarding pass, I proceeded to weigh my baggage. I felt quite anxious, worried about whether its weight may cross the limit. Next, I handed over my passport and boarding pass to an immigration officer. He looked at my passport, smiled, and said, "You are from Kashmir, it is your first time going abroad," to which I replied, "Yes Sir." He handed back my passport with a final note and said, "Jawo beta, yaha pe kuch nahi rakha." ("Go son. There's nothing left here."). After clearing immigration, I called my family to speak with them one last time before leaving India. The boarding announcement was made, and as I settled into my seat and fastened my seatbelt, it was time for takeoff. I was ready to bid "alvida" to Delhi and greet Paris with a heartfelt "Bonjour".

Chapter - 2

Around midnight, the pilot announced takeoff, sending a wave of unease through me. I experienced unprecedented fear, stemming from the strangeness of this experience and anxiety about potential mishaps. The flight was noticeably more comfortable than India's "flying buses", featuring better interiors and functional screens in front of each seat. Minute details like complimentary rugs and earphones captivated my attention as domestic flights in India don't offer such facilities. Throughout the flight, I noticed only a few French or other foreign passengers while the majority appeared to be from India.

About an hour into the flight, the attendants began serving snacks. For the first time, I was surprised to see a middle-aged female flight attendant with slight wrinkles on her face. However, the real surprise came later when I noticed a bald male flight attendant, likely in his late 50s, serving meals. Unlike India, where the preference often leans towards younger women, typically in their mid-20s to 30s, for such roles. After another hour and a half, one of the air hostesses approached our row with the food tray. Unsure if the food was halal, I chose the vegetarian option as I was hesitant to ask. After the first meal, the lights were dimmed and everyone wrapped their rugs over their shoulders, some slept while others kept watching movies on their respective screens. Struggling to sleep, I started playing with the screen, choosing to watch a movie to pass the time. Later in the night, another meal was served, the cabin lights were dimmed again, and although I felt dizzy, I couldn't fall asleep. Mid-flight, I got up to go to the washroom while still half-asleep. When the washroom door wouldn't open, I noticed a hinge at the top, mistakenly thinking it was the lock. I pulled it down, and the door swung open on both sides, jolting me from my grogginess to full alertness. Realizing my mistake, I felt a rush of shock and embarrassment as a flight attendant explained, in a very French demeanour, that "it wasn't a lock" and that I needed to push the door forcefully to open it. I rushed to another washroom, still in a state of shock, and returned to my seat filled with shame and worry about a possible fine. Now the toilet door remained wide open throughout the journey, offering nearby passengers an unexpected and unfiltered view of something they had likely never imagined witnessing on a flight. After remaining in a state of torpor for a few more hours, my relief grew as no one approached me about the incident.

It was just ten minutes before the flight was due to land when I caught my first glimpse of France from the air. The flight landed around 6 A.M, and the weather was misty and cold. Our arrival involved numerous formalities, including a rapid test for COVID-19. After the security check, I connected my smartphone to the airport Wi Fi and contacted my driver, who had been arranged by the master's program I was enrolled in. He texted me the gate number. With the help of some security personnel, I managed to reach there and saw a person in a black suit at the gate holding a sign with my name, 'M. KHAN,' on his iPad screen. He was waiting for me and asked me to hand over my luggage. At that moment, I felt rather important, and as we headed towards the car, which was nothing but a Mercedes, I was in a state of disbelief but also feeling nervous about being so far from home. The sun had not fully risen, and the weather was still hazy. I showed my driver the address of my residence and asked him about the duration of our journey. In his French accent, he said, 'Oui, one hour,' and we started heading towards the suburbs of Paris.

Just as the sun was about to fully emerge, I reached my residence. Priya, a PhD student from the same university, was there to welcome me. A friend from India introduced me to her, and she assisted me in finding the accommodation. She introduced me to my landlady, Alexandra, who was also waiting there to hand over the keys of my room. Alexandra, in her seventies, seemed a bit surprised to see me.

Expecting a typical Indian boy, she instead met a full-bearded man with a light skin tone, looking more Afghan or Persian than Indian. She touched my beard with both hands and smiled before handing me the keys. After settling in, Priya had prepared a vegetarian meal for me. During our somewhat shy conversation, as I struggled to make an eye contact, she frequently used the word "salla" for the far-right politicians in India. Initially, I thought I misheard, but her repeated use of the word confirmed it was intentional. She was very kind and suggested visiting the Eiffel Tower on my very first day. I agreed, although I knew my feelings for this famous monument were about to change. She mentioned that the train ticket would cost ten euros, so I handed her the cash, and we headed to the station. Hearing her speak mediocre French with the train employee impressed me, and I started dreaming of speaking French fluently. We boarded the RER B train, and after a 45-minute journey, I finally got the chance to see the monument that I had only seen on TV screens and text books. My first impression was, 'It's okay,' but too overrated. It was a modest steel structure with a muted brown hue, undergoing renovation at the time. As I looked at the view, I couldn't help but think of the Taj Mahal, which, in my eyes, seemed to have a beauty that was hard to rival. But as the lights of the tower illuminated the night, the view became absolutely mesmerizing and breathtaking. We sat in the park, looking at the tower, and during our conversation, Priya talked about her relationship and asked if I had a girlfriend. My answer was straightforward but very surprising to her. I told her that I see her and every girl as my sister. She seemed a bit annoyed and replied, 'Even the one you are going to marry?' I explained, 'I say sister out of respect, not because I am related to someone.' After reflecting for a while, she finally began to grasp what I meant. After spending some more time there, we decided to head back since I needed to prepare for classes the next day.

In the evening, I took on another painstaking task of preparing a meal for myself. Having never ventured into the kitchen before, not even during my time in Aligarh, I had always preferred the simplicity of washing dishes over the complexity of preparing a meal with friends. So, for the first time, I prepared something simple, a vegetable mix of potatoes and onions. It took me around two hours to cook. My eyes were filled with tears from chopping the onions. The outcome of my tireless and naive cooking was good as it tasted much better than expected. To bring out the maximum flavour, I made sure to mix in every Indian and

Pakistani spices into the food, without paying much attention to the quantity. Due to my limited cooking skills, I also tried many unusual experiments, such as making an omelet with Algerian sauce and adding peanuts to the curry. These odd but enlightening activities improved my skills over time. The next morning, I received an email from the course coordinator advising me to stay home for the next two days as a precautionary measure to prevent the spread of the coronavirus. I began attending classes online, just like I had been doing in India. Upon checking my course schedule, I realized that my French language class was scheduled to be held in a different building located on another part of the campus. I looked up the route to the building where the class would be held, and the following morning, I boarded BUS 91 without a ticket in hand. Hesitantly, I handed a ten - euro bill to the driver, who looked at me and said, "No change." Unsure of the fare, I asked a fellow passenger who looked like a student. He handed me some coins in exchange for my 10- euro bill. When I noticed he was a few coins short, I smiled and said, "No worries, keep it." His expression froze in disbelief, as though I'd just performed a heroic act instead of letting go of a few cents.

About ten minutes later, I arrived at the building, which looked like a massive modern structure straight out of a Hollywood movie, capable of accommodating several villages together. The facilities like vending machines, unique seating arrangements, and eye-catching lights and interior design, were incredibly fascinating to me. I followed a group of students and eventually stumbled upon my class. It was a diverse assembly of people from different departments, each expressing their unique personalities through their different styles. Some sported piercings and tattoos, exuding a bold vibe, while others were wearing oversized, baggy outfits, giving off the vibe of a hip-hop crew. Their intriguing appearances immediately caught my attention, but as it turned out, none of them were actually in my master's program. The lecture began, and the professor, who appeared to be in her late fifties, had barely combed her grayish-blonde hair and had a wrinkled face. It was her second or third lecture, and she started by directly asking students their names in French. I began to tremble inside, confused, as I had no idea what she was going to ask. When she said, "Comment' appelles-tu?", a Vietnamese student before me said, "Kay," which I knew was his name because he had told me before the lecture. When the professor asked me the same question, I quickly replied, "Haziq." She nodded her head and said, "Très bien" Which translates to "alright".

The next morning, after a brief quarantine, I was finally able to attend my main classes in person and meet my classmates. Despite the rain, I made sure to leave early to arrive on time. I walked and used Google Maps to locate bâtiment 440, where my classes were being held. This was my first time using this app. While walking, the map directed me through lanes that made me feel as though I was entering someone's home. While still figuring out which way to go, I saw a girl with a backpack looking like a pupil of the same university. I asked her about the university and my building. She pointed towards the dense jungle in front of us and said, "This is the university," and she did not know the whereabouts of the building.

The view of the university shrouded in a forest with no buildings in sight, evoked the sensation of entering a forgotten land from which there was no return. As I walked along the road, I eventually reached Bâtiment 440, distinguished by the Erasmus Mundus logo. The moment I stepped inside, a wave of nervousness swept over me. I ascended one floor after another, and my anxiety rose proportionally. I made my way to the social room, where I met a few of my classmates, a girl from the Middle East, and several students from Asian and European backgrounds. There was no formal welcome, everyone seemed preoccupied with their assignments and lab reports, leaving me clueless about the academic challenges ahead.

In the classroom, the diversity was striking, with students from America, Italy, Spain, and various African, Asian, and Arab countries. It became clear from the first lecture that this experience wouldn't be a walk in the park. Professors were already discussing midterm exams scheduled two weeks away and providing details about the upcoming lab sessions, each lasting either a full day or half a day over the next three months. The following day, on a misty morning, I joined my group mates for our first lab session on mass spectrometry, a technique we barely knew existed. Faced with equipment worth loads of dollars, our professor instructed us to operate it directly, without any sufficient prior instruction. Despite our apprehension and skepticism, we managed to complete our first lab session by repeatedly asking for her assistance. The report was due in one week. Later that day, I needed to arrange my SIM card and open a bank account in the nearby branch. Since I couldn't speak French, another classmate offered to help me buy a SIM card from the "tabac" shop.

The next day, we were given a class test in the organic chemistry course. Professor Nicole, whose name was feared by all students, possessed a moody Parisian demeanor. The test went very poorly for me, and my grades reflected that. His lectures were scientifically commendable, but his harsh behavior toward students was creating hitches in maintaining a fearless rapport with the teachers. Additionally, my interaction with classmates revealed gaps in my scientific approaches and exposure. For most of them, these courses were like any other they had already taken. While the level of difficulty seemed manageable to them, some expressed concerns about the tight schedule and the complexity of the subjects. I felt like a sheep among wolves, completely out of place and left out, but my faith in Allah reignited hope within me.

A few days later, another lab session paired me with two girls, both from Europe, one Ukrainian and the other Polish. As assignments, exams, and classwork converged, my daily schedule became chaotic, disrupting my daily prayers, meals, and escalating my stress exponentially. As the submission deadline approached, tensions arose during the report preparations. For the first time, I used Google Docs, which helped us to work online simultaneously from our respective residences. Although I initially took on the writing tasks and started with the introduction, it was because they weren't very proficient in English, and it seemed like a great opportunity for me to contribute in some way. I did my best to maximize my contribution, but handling the technical aspect, such as graph analysis, was incredibly challenging for me. As a result, I focused on revising the calculations, and the textual part was completed by the Ukrainian girl. Despite my efforts, my contributions didn't seem to impress and were considered inadequate, especially by the Ukrainian girl. Near the project's completion, she threatened to remove my name from the report unless I provided a fair reason for my perceived lack of contribution, which she communicated rudely in the WhatsApp group created by the three of us. This statement felt like a challenge to my self-respect. The Polish girl, whose contribution was similar to mine, started supporting her. I responded politely, explaining my situation and mentioning my problem due to personal issues, but she seemed unsympathetic and replied that she would be deducting my name from the report. My response was "Do as you like," but deep inside, I was optimistic that she would not follow through after realizing that I had only recently arrived.

My hope of staying in France started to dwindle as the days passed. A week later, while walking to attend my French classes, I learned from the Polish girl that my name had indeed been removed from the report. I was shattered and speechless, and my despair deepened because I couldn't possibly pass my course without the lab grades. Upon returning to my room, I had a distressing phone conversation with my family, explaining my situation and mentioning that it might be possible for me to come back.

Just before the mid-term exams, the stress and anxiety reached such a pinnacle that I finally decided to give up and leave France. I convinced my family, although my mother and brother were deeply concerned about my health and mental well-being. They said, "We need you, not your degree." My father, on the other hand, agreed with my decision but also tried to boost my morale by mentioning the incident of the Muslim army's expedition to Spain, where the leader ordered the boats to be burned to eliminate the possibility of retreat, encouraging me to either succeed or fail without surrendering. My other friends, both in Aligarh and France, were also trying to change my mind and withdraw from the decision to go back to Kashmir, but the effect of their advice on me was very minuscule considering the situations I was facing. Despite everyone's concern for me, the overwhelming stress and anxiety pushed me to the brink of departure. Just as I was arranging my exit through the embassy online, a small relief came in the form of my first paycheck of 1,200 euros, providing a temporary respite from my financial worries.

On Friday, I was preparing to attend the sermon at the nearby mosque and decided to skip classes from then on. As I was getting ready to leave for prayer and on my way back, a renewed sense of hope began to surface in my mind. I considered staying at least until the end of the semester's final exams in January, despite my fears of failure. This thought offered a glimmer of hope amidst the overwhelming challenges, though my faith in *"taqdeer"* always balanced my skepticism.

Now the mid-term exams had started. I worked to the best of my ability, but after looking at the previous year's exam paper, I realized that my comprehension skills were not meeting the level of the questions, especially in the quantum chemistry course. Unlike in India, we were not granted any holidays for exam preparation. The situation worsened after the exam schedule was announced, and to our dismay, we were surprised to find that we had two or even three exams scheduled per day. The exam period was very hectic but passed by quickly. It suddenly made me nostalgic for the cosy days at Aligarh, where the court members or any politically active student would postpone the exam dates until every student in the class agreed. That "*dealing*" felt like a magic spell that every Alig cherished.

After navigating the first daunting hurdle of the quantum chemistry exam, I gained confidence by exceeding my expectations, having initially predicted my grades would be zero. Although our professor allowed us to bring formulas written on a piece of paper, answering the questions required far more knowledge and understanding than what an A4-sized cheat sheet could provide. The subsequent exams followed one after another, and in the electrochemistry exam, I finished my paper ahead of time and went home feeling somewhat relieved. Little did I know that this relief would be very short-lived.

In the evening, just as I was about to sleep, I glanced at the question paper again and realized my blunder. As I turned the sheet over, more questions appeared before my eyes. I had forgotten to look to the other side and completely ignored the additional questions. The moment left me stunned, and it felt as though my ability to see and think had come to a

halt. The sudden realization urged me to send an email to the professor that same night, to which he responded rather thoughtlessly. Fear began to overwhelm me, and the tides of failure seemed to surface over my head, but I remained resolute in my decision to stay.

Just after our midterm session concluded, we had to form groups again for biophysics lab reports, and there was only one person left to pair with, the same Ukrainian girl who had removed my name from the report previously. I was already embittered by her cruel nature, but this time, I made sure not to take any chances. I took charge and completed all three reports with better contribution and technicality.

Life continued like this, unending report submissions, day-long classes, poor time management, and, above all, onerous exams. On the other hand, the scientific approach of most of my peers was significantly better than mine. Many of them had an efficient working style and were adept at applying concepts simultaneously. This difference was deeply rooted in their extensive exposure to European culture and the strong, high-quality education system of their home countries.

A few weeks later, the results of our midterm exams were announced, and they were just as expected, barely on the borderline of failure. I was too shy to talk about my results. The university administration used to keep our results encrypted since the grades were sent via email, so no one else would know them except the recipient. However, I was quite curious about the scores of my mates, and they seemed just as interested. While texting to some of my classmates, in the middle of our conversation, I would ask them about their grades. As far as I knew, some students performed exceptionally well in certain subjects, while others received scores similar to mine.

Knowing that others had similar performances gave me the courage to work harder. And sometimes, a persistent fear also haunted me, I was petrified of how the people I knew would react if I returned home. It felt like walking a tightrope, with these thoughts swirling around me, trying to swoon me, and the constant fear of falling always lingering beneath. The expectations from family and friends only added to the pressure. After the mid-semester, I decided to change my study approach. It no longer seemed important to spend hours on the teacher's presentations since there was little to learn or retain from the slides. The focus had shifted to applying concepts rather than memorizing them. As I adopted this approach, my final grades started to drop even further. The lack of guidance, combined with feelings of isolation and peer pressure, worsened the situation. During this peak of tensity, many students in my class still found time to socialize and enjoy themselves, which baffled me when it came to time management. I was quite introverted at that time, and experiencing cultural novelty prevented me from socializing with them. It also didn't motivate me to join their social groups or attend parties. I got to know some classmates during the formation of lab groups, but there were many with whom I never spoke throughout the entire semester. Despite these challenges, one thing that lifted my spirits was knowing that my scholarship amount was more substantial than any of the ones my classmates received.

Meanwhile, Asim and I were nearing the end of the first semester at our respective universities, while Wajid was still facing issues with his visa. He was extremely stressed, and his hopes of coming to France were fading. It is incredibly challenging to endure when your peers have already completed half of their semester, and your visa officer is still demanding more documents from you. Wajid grew increasingly depressed, feeling as if each passing day was like sleeping on burning coals. The irony of fate was that he, the first among us to receive the SSGA scholarship, remained stuck in limbo. He stayed in Delhi with his baggage packed, having already bid farewell to his parents, hopeful that his visa would arrive any day. Days turned into weeks, and weeks into months, yet there was no word from the visa office. Eventually, he returned home and began assisting his uncle in an election campaign in their home constituency. It was as if he had enough and had withdrawn from the decision to go to France. Wajid became deeply involved, taking charge of arrangements and became the main organizer of his uncle's entourage. When the election results were announced, Wajid was moved to tears, his uncle had won the seat. This news felt like a gentle breeze of happiness for him. A few days later, after a delay of two and a half months, Wajid finally received his visa to France. Human perception is where you aspire to be, but *taqdeer* (fate) decides where you end up. His visa approval was nothing short of gratifying news for us, and we celebrated it like never before. However, we were also concerned about how he would manage his final exams after such a prolonged delay.

After the Christmas break, our final exams began with the same intensity and crowded atmosphere. We completed the exams in the first week of January, although I wasn't sure about my results. For the other students who weren't part of the Erasmus mobility program like me, had to remain at the same university, while others were going to complete their second semester in different European countries. Our second semester started so swiftly that it felt like another release of Akshay Kumar's movie. It started even before announcing the final grades of the first semester. The majority of our classmates left and only four of us remained to complete our second semester in France.

We didn't get any break after finishing our final exams, the second semester's lectures started out of nowhere. We were also expecting our first-semester grades to be released that month, but I wasn't sure if I'd pass or if I'd have to retake the semester or worse, return home. One morning, I woke up and checked my smartphone, where I found an email from the course coordinator. It was about the final results. This email felt like a small window of either hope or despair for me. My hands started to shiver as if "chilya kalan" (The harsh winter period in Kashmir) has hit on me, and my heart began to race fast. It felt like I had already failed and was preparing to leave France. As I anxiously scanned for my student number, I saw the final column showing that I had qualified. My eyes rained with emotions, and I performed *Sajda-e-Shukr* (prostration of thanks). I took my phone and called my family; their happiness had no limits either.

This period made me realize the profound importance of faith (Iman) and family. Allah has bestowed these two precious gifts upon us, but many of us fail to recognize their value until we face adversity. I also came to understand, why I struggled so much as a student of chemistry, despite having graduated from a top-ranked university in India. The reasons were clear, the way we are taught and the way we learn are far from what is required by the modern educational system. Moreover, our dependency on each other as Aligs, even for itsy-bitsy matters, erodes our resilience and hinders the development of essential skills.

The second semester marked a new beginning, but I was still unsure of how to proceed. We began studying courses that were new to me. Although the courses were as challenging as those in the first semester, the session was shorter because of an additional two-month internship that was required to be completed to validate the M1. Fortunately, in one of our courses, we had the privilege of meeting one of the great tutors Mr. Pirad, a unique and hardworking lecturer. He taught us the Photo physics course, and his teaching style was distinctive. He kept the students engaged and actively involved with tasks throughout his lectures. We never got bored because his interactive approach actively improved our critical thinking and scientific mindset. Along with Professor Rebecca, who was also creative and encouraged dynamic thinking, they pushed us to critically analyze the published research articles. Professor Rebecca would hand out articles during the lecture and test us to identify mistakes, which was difficult at first, but it planted the seeds of critical thinking and a solid research approach in our minds. Mr. Pirad further boosted our morale in the field of research by encouraging us to publish a research article.

My acquaintance with the system began to grow, and I gradually started to feel somewhat confident, although I still lacked a full understanding of how things were done. I slowed down and began studying more like a typical European student, which essentially meant dedicating less time to my studies than before. Time flew by, and within three months, our final exams for the second semester began. However, this time I felt less stressed than before. I passed the exams with better grades, but there was still a noticeable gap between me and the other students.

In the month of May, I began my M1 internship with a French supervisor, which lasted for about two months. My work focused on nanoscience, and it was my first experience working in a research lab. I felt a mix of curiosity and nervousness due to my inexperience as an intern. During that period, I was co-supervised by a female PhD student from India. The first week as an intern was spent being cautious and trying not to break any glassware, but gradually, things began to fall into place. The instructions from my French supervisor were like watching a Chinese movie with Korean subtitles. she had been developing her ideas for years, and I often felt caught between her words and my interpretation. I would take notes as thoroughly as possible while listening to her and then interpret her words in the lab. During the internship, I was introduced to some powerful techniques, such as the Transmission Electron Microscope (TEM), which was very fascinating to me at that time.

My work appeared to be progressing well, and the experimental results were also promising. The internship required a report to be submitted, along with a presentation where I had to defend my thesis. As the thesis submission deadline loomed, I found myself working relentlessly on my internship report, often writing late into the night. While my supervisor's feedback was limited due to the heavy administrative responsibilities placed on her, which understandably shifted her focus from scientific research to management duties, she was unable to review my report effectively. During my thesis presentation, the referee pointed out several mistakes, which I acknowledge were partly my fault. However, the experience taught me resilience and emphasized the importance of seeking guidance proactively. In the end, I successfully finished my M1 with average grades, which, at that time, felt like a significant achievement for me.

In the meantime, both my friends in Dijon (France), Wajid and Asim, faced another setback. They had a few backlogs in their second semester, which could potentially ruin their entire year. Their scholarship was also suspended, and the fear of returning to India began to overshadow them. We had a conference call, and they looked pale, with the happiness gone from their faces. They were struggling with both financial and mental stress, but in the end, they passed the semester, albeit at the cost of losing their scholarship. Later, they managed their expenses by taking on difficult side hustles, such as elbowing their way into construction jobs as laborers. Despite these challenging circumstances, they had one humongous blessing that I lacked, having many Alig brothers around at the same university. Several Alig seniors, like Fazil Bhai, were very supportive and social. That was something I deeply missed, as not having anyone to talk to for an extended period can be quite disturbing and depressing. After they passed their exams, it was a great relief not just for them, but for all of us. We genuinely thought of ourselves as brothers and cared for one another for the sake of Allah.

When we were nearing the completion of M1, we also used to call Mujtaba, and he often used to display his enthusiasm for studying abroad. At that time, while pursuing his Master's at AMU (India), Mujtaba was doing everything possible, leaving no stone unturned and diligently filling out international scholarship applications. He began attending his master's classes remotely due to the pandemic, while also reaching out to professors for recommendation letters. His struggle was fueled both by his zeal and the inspiration that he had drawn from peers who were already in Europe.

At the end of the first year and after completing all the laborious and mind-bending tasks, it was finally time to rest and relax. The summer vacation began, and at first, it felt very peaceful and easy. However, as the days passed, the monotonous routine of just sleeping and eating made life feel stagnant. This period was more difficult to endure than the hectic class schedule of the M1 courses. So, I decided to visit Turkey. I flew there in the last week of July, traveling alone with just a single backpack. As soon as I landed at the airport, my first glimpse of Istanbul was like stepping into a fairytale. I immediately fell in love with the city, the breathtaking view of the Bosporus with its blue waters, the grandeur of Ottoman mosques, the friendly people, and the cheap yet delicious cuisine all captivated me. I exchanged euros for lira at the airport, and seeing the amount in my hand, which was tenfold higher than the euro, I thought I could manage the entire trip on that sum. However, contrary to my expectations, my pocket was empty by the evening.

The city was full of life, bustling with people everywhere. I felt a strong connection to the city, and the people seemed friendly too. I visited the

Hagia Sophia mosque prayed there and saw a text inscribed on the stone plate explaining how Constantinople was handed to Muslims by Christians. During my visit, I met a Caucasian nurse from the Balkans. While she shared her experiences of living in Turkey, she also spoke about the racism she encountered there. To my surprise, I found myself wondering how a blonde woman as white as snow could face racism. She explained, "They call us *'white crows.'*" I was taken aback for a moment and then began to consider it might be true, as Turkish people seemed very fashionable, with high beauty standards that led many women to undergo plastic surgery.

Even though Turkey is a Muslim-majority country, the visible presence of Islam was not as prevalent as I expected. Alcohol consumption and other activities were widespread in Istanbul. Those who are religious are often affiliated with Sufism, and it is common to visit graves and pay homage to Sufi saints and their shrines. One time, while walking by the Bosphorus, I noticed people dancing and being busy taking photos. Later that evening, I went to pray Maghrib at the Fatih Mosque, where I witnessed a non-Muslim girl taking her Shahada and embracing Islam. The moment filled me with immense joy. As I left the mosque, I reflected on the profound choices people make in life. Regardless of one's upbringing, whether born into an atheist family or a practicing Muslim family, each individual has the freedom to choose their path. Some may devote themselves to Allah, while others may pursue different lifestyles. This solo trip offered valuable insights and broadened my understanding of different types of people and cultures. I returned to Paris after an 11-day journey, full of stories to share about my experiences in Istanbul.

After gaining all this experience, I began to reflect on how people from various countries, cultures, and ethnicities perceive others and interact with those from different backgrounds. With the diverse backgrounds of my classmates, I already had an acquaintance with the idea that the way of thinking shifts dynamically from culture to culture. Most of the Western European countries can be put into a single pot. Their criteria for decision-making, their ways of entertainment, and socialization are very similar. The differences may include the kind of food and the language, but most of them are still united on pasta, pizza, and English. Many people in these countries are open to learning new languages and cultures, unless chauvinism arises, such as tension between France and the United Kingdom or viewing a non-European language as inferior.

The color of your skin, nationality, superficial confidence, playing it cool, fake smiling, wealth, the brand of your clothes, the fragrance of your perfume, being good at drinking and smoking, your speech and accent, a preference for food without spices, being irreligious, speaking about social taboos while avoiding discussion of ongoing major genocidal events, having tattoos and body piercings, and lacking certain traditionally masculine features like a beard are some traits that can significantly influence interactions with European people or those of Western mindset. Racism is also widespread in Europe, with foreigners frequently encountering it through verbal remarks and discriminatory actions. In France, there are racist slurs for various ethnicities, such as "Bamboula" for Black people, "Annamite" for Vietnamese, "Beurette" for Arabs, and "Paki" for Indians and Pakistanis. Their behavior can often make foreigners feel strange and offensive. Additionally, they tend to prefer speaking in French, and they may be reluctant to offer help or guidance if you're lost or need of any sort assistance.

Despite being a cosmopolitan part of the world, the language barrier can prevent you from fully understanding French or European society as a whole.

The lack of interactions with locals, along with their reluctance to speak English coupled with our own hesitance to learn their language, reinforces this divide. Parisians, in particular, often epitomize their chutzpah, displaying an air of self-assuredness not just toward foreigners but also toward non-Parisians from other regions of France.

The communities who reside in France like North Africans, primarily Arabs and Berbers, as well as other people from across Africa, including those from the Black community, share cultural, moral, and culinary similarities with people from the Indian subcontinent. Many Arab Muslims from these regions are known for their soft nature, helpfulness, and hospitality. This virtue is especially evident among individuals who have not been influenced by the notions of superiority that can sometimes emerge from living in or being born in Europe.

People from other Asian countries, particularly China, tend to be shy yet polite in their speech and are often helpful, especially if you have extended some sort of assistance to them. People from countries like Pakistan, Bangladesh, and India often share a sense of camaraderie and are generally welcoming, especially when their shared cultural and religious values align with each other. However, other students from India do not always exhibit the same sense of community. They often prefer to keep to themselves, avoiding interaction with newly arrived Indian students and not readily offering help. Some Indian students abroad have leaned toward far-right ideologies, especially following political changes in India, which can lead to noticeable hostility even after brief interactions.

Nevertheless, many other Indian students who are honest and kind exhibit a strong sense of empathy, particularly towards persecuted minorities in India.

European cuisine, on the other hand, is often viewed by all the other communities including Arabs, Indians, Pakistanis, Africans, and Chinese as less flavorful but aesthetically well-presented. They feel it doesn't align with their taste preferences, primarily due to the lack of spices, and, in some cases, the excessive use of butter, particularly in the French cuisine. This may be attributed to the fact that European countries historically have not cultivated spices extensively, and their cuisine has traditionally lacked these ingredients. They claim that this approach preserves the authentic taste of the food without wavering it with abundant spices. At student restaurants, the food is typically simple, prioritizing sustenance over enjoyment. There are two options in student restaurants: vegetarian, which may also include fish, and the second option is meat, which includes beef, pork, and chicken, with no halal option. Despite all the criticisms, Turkish doner kebabs and tacos have maintained a good standard of taste for foreigners. There are also Michelin-star restaurants where each meal can cost well over 50 euros, which is simply unaffordable for an average person. However, this downside was a blessing in disguise, as it encouraged me to cook for myself. Within just the span of one year, I could prepare many different meals with exceptional, if not superb, taste. The availability of halal meat in Paris is not a concern, as Muslim butcher shops are very common. This is due to the large Muslim population in France, which is among the highest in Western Europe.

Due to the significant Muslim population in France, the relationship between Muslims and the broader French society is an important topic to address. Many Muslims in France come from North African countries such as Morocco, Algeria, and Tunisia, as well as sub - Saharan African nations like Senegal, Mali, and Ivory Coast, which were once French colonies. This colonial rule had a profound impact on their cultures. French is often spoken as a second language in these countries, and beyond language, French cultural influences are evident, particularly in areas such as clothing. For instance, many had adopted European styles of dress. Some male individuals are also influenced by aspects of the French lifestyle, such as drinking alcohol or participating in nightlife. However, the majority continue to identify as Muslims, with varying degrees of religious observance, from very devout to non- practicing. One notable contrast is seen in some Muslim females who adopt European-style clothing, such as wearing skirts, yet observe Islamic practices like fasting during Ramadan. Similarly, many Muslim women wear hijab paired with jeans and makeup. These mixed expressions of faith and fashion are common in France. Some Muslims who observe the proper attire may struggle with understanding Islamic aqeedah (creed) with their sense of right and wrong, influenced more by modern norms than by the teachings of Islam. Many Muslims in France face challenges integrating into French society, often encountering resistance from some French people who may exclude them from closed social circles, sometimes due to underlying prejudices or discriminatory attitudes. Afro-French Muslims, in particular, face heightened levels of racism, exacerbating these difficulties.

A crucial topic that needs to be addressed as well is how people from our communities, in particular, face challenges and how their behavior is perceived by others.

All these difficulties faced by the foreigners in Europe can also be explained by the term "culture shock." Culture shock can be generally defined by four stages: (1) Honeymoon stage, (2) Anxiety stage, (3) Acceptance stage, and (4) Adaptation stage. However, for a student, the first stage of comfort is bypassed, and the journey often begins with anxiety, which typically peaks during the first five to six months. Over time, the student realizes that these challenges are not going away and starts to accept them as they are. Adaptation begins when the individual settles down with a decent job and, in some cases, becomes a citizen of the host country. The arrival of any student from the subcontinent, who gradually learns to cope with challenges over time, often brings exposure to new trials and fitnahs. Initially, some of us, upon seeing an interracial couple, a Black man and a Caucasian woman are struck with heart-halting shock, mistakenly thinking we might also have a chance, which is nothing but beating around the bush. The Western environment brings about noticeable changes in male students, who often adopt pro-feminist behaviors to fit in the circles of female students. Meanwhile, the female students begin to present themselves as strong and independent, except when seeking assistance from male peers. Many students attempt to integrate into social groups where partying and drinking are common, and, in some cases, they indulge in activities which they once viewed as taboos.

Male students coming to Europe for studies often face significant challenges, particularly those with limited exposure, who are reasonably smart and hold traditional cultural beliefs. Upon arrival, they frequently find themselves alone, without anyone to greet them at the airport or assist with their needs. This can lead to feelings of isolation, especially if they don't conform to the contemporary standards of socialization, a challenge that can differ from the experiences of female students. The low self-esteem observed among some male students can be attributed to factors such as limited exposure, weak financial backgrounds, lack of language fluency, perceived unattractiveness, and a different culture that places high value on breaking social taboos. In contrast, some girls from the subcontinent may arrive with a sense of confidence and self-worth, gently influenced by the culture of appreciation on social media and the polite interaction they experience while abroad.

Many of these young men come to study in Europe, not out of a desire to explore or share their experiences on social media, but due to the heavy burden of family responsibilities. There are also differences in how scholarship money is managed. While many of the students, if not all, may save and spend their funds primarily on themselves, some students often feel pressured to prioritize family needs over personal ones, leading them to economize on their expenses.

The superfluous attention given to certain colleagues, either by seniors or their peers has become a concern, as it may unintentionally elevate their status, potentially leading to overly confident or self-assured behavior. Messages from female newbies in the WhatsApp group often receive immediate attention and enthusiastic responses from male students, who are quick to offer help or answer questions. On the other hand, messages from male students sometimes go unnoticed, akin to the preface of a book that many tend to skip over. This disparity in engagement can inadvertently create an imbalance, leading to a sense of division between those eager to assist female students and those who remain indifferent.

When describing individuals and their personalities from different regions across the globe, it is essential to recognize that our perceptions are often shaped by our own mental frameworks, biases, and attitudes toward those cultures or groups. These preconceived notions can significantly influence how we interpret others' behaviors, traits, and values. This can be elaborated by the fact that people from different regions of India are also judged by various stereotypes. For example, people from Bihar are stereotyped as backward, even though Bihar has a rich history and significant intellectual contributions. People from South India are termed as "Madrasi," which is a very simplified version of the cultures of the southern states. Northeasterners are victims of racism and are often mistaken to be foreigners because of their different physical features. Punjabis, who are otherwise known for their hospitality and warmth, are stereotyped as loud, showy, or overly fond of food and celebrations.

Understanding this dynamic is crucial, as it highlights the importance of self-awareness and the need to approach such discussions with empathy and openness. This is a nuanced and an important topic that deserves careful attention. Below are some observations that shed light on this complex interplay of perception and personality

Africans: They are among the kindest and most diligent people I have ever met. Unfortunately, there is a tendency among some individuals to exhibit racist behavior towards African people, often using derogatory terms like "kallu," which translates to "black." Such behavior is unacceptable and perpetuates harmful stereotypes.

Chinese: While interactions with Chinese people are generally polite, certain prejudices persist, particularly concerning their cuisine. The term "chinki" is sometimes used derogatorily by Indians, which is highly inappropriate and offensive. Despite these biases, Chinese people are often viewed favorably in social contexts, second only to Arabs.

Europeans: The personalities and ways of thinking among Europeans vary significantly. They differ in terms of politics, economy, food, and social interactions with people from abroad. However, there is often a tendency by the people of the sub-continent to perceive Europeans as the epitome of human civilization, which can sometimes lead to belittling native cultural practices due to comparison. Initially, meeting a white foreigner may feel like an adrenaline rush, filled with excitement. However, over time, people come to realize that skin color is irrelevant when it comes to meaningful social interactions.

French: Interactions with French people can sometimes be challenging due to cultural misunderstandings. These misunderstandings might lead to behaviors that could be perceived as unfriendly or distant, but this is often a result of differences in communication styles. French are often perceived as less approachable and are frequently regarded by other Europeans and non-Europeans as being prideful.

Italians: Italians are known for their humor and relaxed attitude but are deeply passionate about their cuisine. Cracking jokes about their food or sometimes their accent, which many find charming, can be perceived as disrespectful.

Spanish and Portuguese: People from Spain and Portugal are generally very warm and welcoming. These countries have diverse populations and also serve as important gateways for migrants. Despite economic difficulties, the people maintain a strong sense of hospitality and pride in their cultural heritage.

Scandinavians, Germans, Swiss, & other small European countries: In these economically prosperous regions, societal values can sometimes feel distant to those from less wealthy nations. Their daily problems are difficult to grasp for third-world countries due to the significant economic gap, which results in differing lifestyles and perspectives. In these regions, women often show stronger support for feminist values, which may also correlate with higher divorce rates.

Balkans, Russians, Ukrainians etc: People from these regions are known for their fair skin and blonde hair, often regarded as some of the most beautiful people in Europe. However, their economies are among the worst hit in Europe as well. Women from this region are frequently admired for their femininity, but unfortunately, harmful stereotypes perpetuated by some Indians have contributed to their offensive and inaccurate portrayal.

Despite the economic achievements in Europe following the Second World War, the social structure remains highly individualistic. The family system, weak to its core, is reflected in their divorce rates which are as high as the ratings of Christopher Nolan's movies. The notion of doing whatever a person likes as long as it doesn't hurt anyone has caused huge blunders and lasting repercussions for European society. The behavior of adults appears less mature and irresponsible, while children seem stressed and burdened, as though they are carrying the weight of the world. Kids under the age of ten are seen vaping, mimicking gang members in their social circles, and bullying one another. The lack of love, guidance, and care from parents and adults, who are preoccupied with their own lives, has caused significant harm to children's behavior and morals.

The older generation, who played a role in establishing the system, is now facing some of its consequences, such as life in old age homes. It is heart-wrenching to see an elderly person in their 80s, confined to a wheelchair, shopping for their groceries. Respect for the elderly and love for the younger generation are rarely seen nowadays. Both young men and women often appear as though they are under the influence, prioritizing pleasure without regard for moral boundaries.

As a result, laws seem to accommodate this system, for instance, people are free to wear semi-nude or fully nude clothing, while modest attire (niqab, hijab, and abaya) is often scrutinized or even banned. The right to choose what to wear only seems to exist when it's not Islamic, as does the right to freedom of speech. They may call for nationwide protests when any crime anywhere in the world involves Muslims, often labeling it as extremism. However, they remain silent or feign ignorance when major genocides occur around the world. This hypocrisy and self- interest are deeply rooted in their colonial mindset, a perspective shaped by historical underpinnings that have been perpetuated through generations. It is unlikely to change anytime soon and will continue to be upheld by the prevailing societal system.

The mind began to grow, yet the heart felt sad,

Life acquired its liberty, but the soul felt entrapped,

And my wish was beautiful but the road was too grueling

Oh, my dear, these are the trails of life which you and I are enduring.

After all the ups and downs, travel experiences, and European enlightenment, my first year in France with my M1 master's program came to an end. With the start of my second year (M2), it kicked off with a piece of good news. Mujtaba, finally received admission offers with two different scholarships, one in Hungary and another in France. When he sought my advice, I recommended France, but deep down, I was skeptical, haunted by the challenges I had faced, and worried he might think of giving up like I did in the beginning. But he eventually chose France, and in 2021, the journey of the two boys came full circle, from being Aligs to becoming Half-Parisians was complete now. The two boys, once lost in their imagination, filled with visions of the bewitching European breeze and pulchritudinous architecture, began to observe the dawn of reality. The sleepless nights and the enduring efforts were finally rewarded with a blissful morning and well-deserved success. In September, as students from various countries started arriving in France, I stood at the Charles de Gaulle Airport holding a white A4-sized sign that read, "Welcome, ITOO," referring to his surname.

A chapter has closed, marking just one step in the journey ahead. With the start of M2, new challenges were about to begin. Now, as one starts to grasp what lies ahead, the act of preparation creates a rhythm filled with anticipation. Problems will arise and continue to do so; what changes is our attitude toward solving them. The evolution of the human brain is firmly based on experience and learning. Belief in *Taqdeer* is key, something people often underestimate, for staying content with what you have and what is yet to come. However, working superficially, without proper guidance, is unlikely to bring any meaningful progress. Advancement in the education system at home is as important as transitioning from a bullock cart to a motor vehicle. A sense of togetherness and sincerity is vital for any bond to remain strong. Change is essential and beneficial, but change from good to bad will negatively impact our lives. Sixty percent of the problems are likely related to our finances, so focus on resolving them, and the remaining 40% will follow. Your principles of righteousness should never be undermined, especially by you. If you believe in them and know they are right, changing them **without rational reasons would be highly unfair.**

Life is a journey from Point A to Point B. Point A is when you were born, and Point B is when you stop growing.

~ **The Author**

www.ingramcontent.com/pod-product-compliance
Lightning Source LLC
LaVergne TN
LVHW061601070526
838199LV00077B/7137